PHILIPPINES POLICE, FIRE & AMBULANCE

PFAC

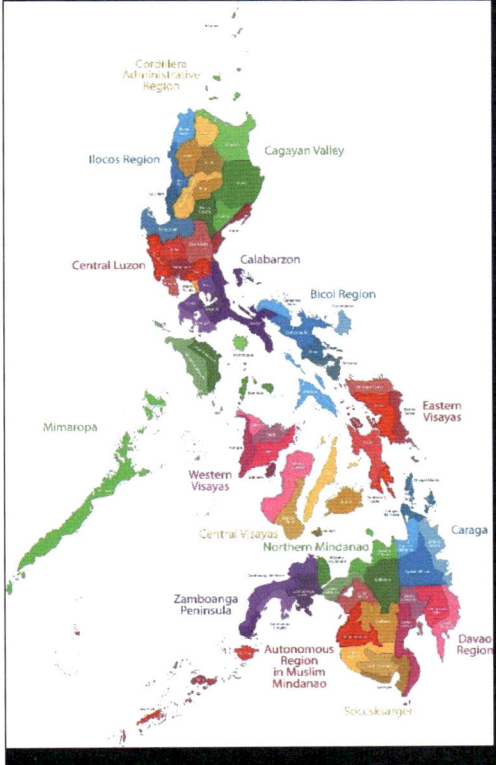

Jonathan lever   www.archilever.com

PFAC for the Philippines: what is the idea behind PFAC, What where, how, why etc – a brief introduction:

I have spent the past almost ten years travelling in and out of the Philippines due to my family, I haven't done as much travelling around the country as I would have like to but I have done some. I have studied the countries infrastructure by default really in my ten years. Being an Architect, its second nature noticing the built environment – and I have a keen interest in things like that anyway.

I have written books regarding healthcare, and hospitals, but this little short coffee time read, is a very focused idea specifically for the Philippines – although it is in many ways applicable to many other countries.

So what I the idea – well the name already pretty much says what it is, so will expand on that. The concept / idea hinges on a countrywide roll out of PFAC centres. Buildings which have under one roof in varying sizes – Police, Fire and Ambulance facilities.

The logic for this comes from very practical observations. In the event of any emergency, be it a large traffic accident, accidents, fires, or unrest of any sort – more often than not all these services are required at once – and not just that, but a systematic co-ordinated response is needed. In terms of actual kit, personnel, skills, co-ordination, services and dealing with the people and situation on the ground.

I believe that there makes a great amount of sense being able to control the initial response from a central hub of sorts – be it in whatever form, size scale. Because you would almost certainly need to block pedestrians, traffic, screen the areas, co-ordinate police, fire and ambulance on any major incident scene. Therefore a central point of data capture and response makes great sense to me.

The chaos of trying to make numerous phone calls and follow ups to three different emergency facilities, then waiting for different time delays etc, is far less efficient than a central point.

The PFAC centres are not replacements for hospitals and hospital ambulance services, nor are they complete replacements for large fire stations. But the PFAC centres can supplement the system well. Each PFAC centre will have minor surgery as well for cuts, bruises, minor stitching.

In the case of an offender receiving minor injuries, the police operations are greatly improved by taking the offender back t0o the PFAC centre for booking and if they need minor treatment they can be sorted out at the centre, rather than wasting police resources with police then having to travel to a central hospital, to sit and wait at a hospital for minor injuries only to come back to the centre.

The PFAC centre will have a small component of medical staff, and fire staff and related equipment and vehicles. Many emergencies require all three services in any case. The numerous fires in built up residential areas, which are common place, often require the combined services of all three emergency services – and are better co-ordinated from a central point. These PFAC centres then will also be linked to call in on resources and staff from other centres.

The PFAC centres will have a colourful vibrant customer services appearance and be there to serve the community – and will also act in a way as tourist service centres and information when needed. They will have a modern, smart look – be well designed and be great Architecture as well.

The Philippines having so many small islands and lots of remote small towns and a very large population to serve, I believe would be well serviced by having thousands of these PFAC centres dotted across the country. It may even make sense to cluster them right next door to 24hr accident emergency centres – the function and use and benefit of the 24hr accident and emergency centres I have well highlighted in a specific book.

I am going to illustrate four types of PFAC centres for this book – there could be any number of sizes and variations, but for the sake of illustrating my concept / idea, three will suffice.

Type 1 is an option where you may want a signature type design, In key tourist areas

Type 2 is an option where you may want Capacity and uses a large shed with facade

Type 3 is an option where you may want a small outpost serving a limited area

Type 4 is an option where you may want a small portable station Where land is an issue. These can be used in Built areas + beaches + Tourist areas.

This option would give a nice image to the public or a well organised service. It would soften the image to the public too, being a community type centre, a place to get help from the police. It would probably have a coffee area too For the public

The building would be recognisable and have a sense of brand and stand out – be visible – physically so, so a beacon, point of reference and easy for people to find and recognise. You can se the training fire tower in the background – these will be great for school visits too

These centres will have a family feel to them and have soft green break out areas for families, wives and kids. In the event of a fire in an area, these break out areas could be temporary displacement areas while help is on its way in terms of temporary accommodation

The fire training tower would also add a huge visual interest for passers by and visits from school kids in the area – over and above being a necessary part of fire training. With these centres being great for school tours, they would inspire kids to looking at becoming A fireman, policeman or ambulance worker later on

The building extends into walls, arches, hard landscaping, forming outdoor area. Greenery and planting essential of course with nice big shady trees. This will immediately soften the ambiance of the centres. Especially for victims of crime coming to a welcoming centre is a big step

Every side of the building will be functional yet beautiful – the fire trucks will need adequate loading and unloading cover area and flow straight onto a green area for training – but visible to the public. We want to create that visual connection and familiarity to these centres

I have created a vibrant logo for these centres – which in effect is like an octopus, with a central point with tentacles reaching out everywhere – or like the sun shining out everywhere. But the logo will be recognisable, vibrant in colours, bold and become a brand – a great way to colour the car park too

I've used a simple bold tower, with the PFAC text and logo standing out clearly – these towers will be at every centre – making them landmark buildings, easy to find, see and get to. The tower design will add vibrancy to the centres too. Maybe a few have a cool feature on them

There needs to be good space for police cars and ambulance arrivals and departure – and these areas can look great too. It would be nice to try get at least some of the centres as award winning designs and put the Philippines on the map with stunning PFAC centres

The car park area can be vibrant and colourful and using the logo design alone would achieve this. I've done here a sculptural looking building. The Philippines is after all a colourful vibrant country – be it in landscape or underwater and culturally in the colours used in fabrics even sails.

I'm of course stating the obvious – but all the services would be operating 24hr a day, not only in the centres, but networked – even the bodycams of emergency responders Can appear on screens at any centre if needed in a crisis.

This option makes a lot of sense when large capacity is needed. Its basically a large warehouse at the back with a pretty wall façade to change the appearance and smarten it up. If you're looking at large roll outs across the country, of course costs are vital. Standard sheds are easy to erect, cost effective. So a set of standard sheds with decorated threshold frontage makes sense to me.

The use of cladding, colours, finishes, designs can rally bring life to a standard shed behind. I have used a raised feature to signal centrality and entrance. The building is bold bright colours too

Here you can see a standard type of warehouse / shed with the façade giving the building a more formal and nice looking frontage to the public. The façade will give the building a more solid stately appearance too. The facade will be a nice design feature to. Bold, colourful

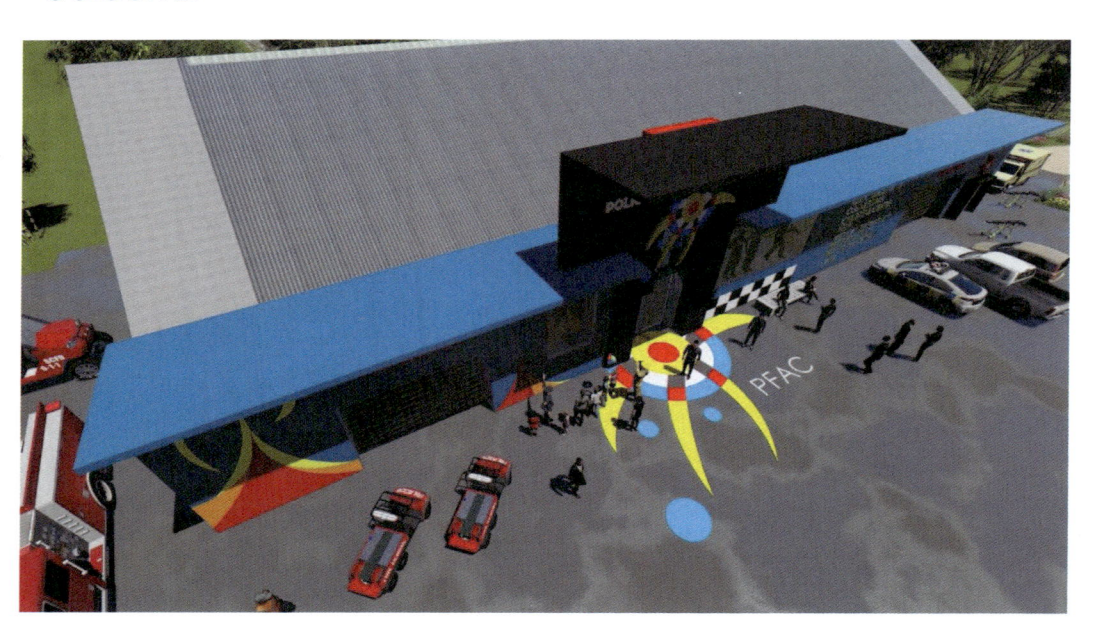

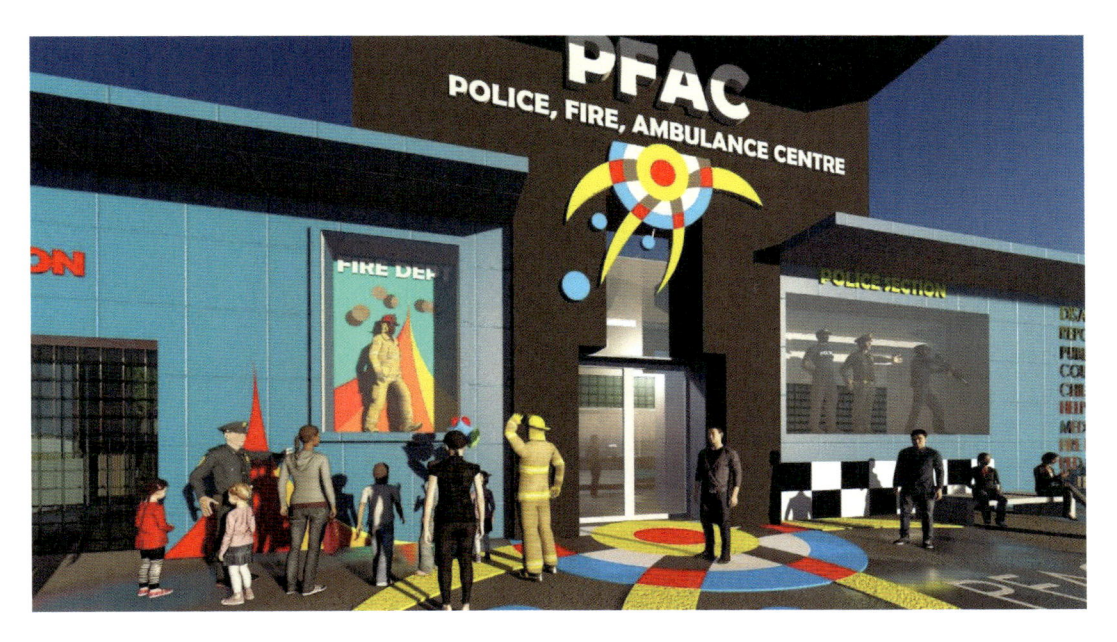

As withal the centres, they will form part of ongoing school visits to give great outings to the school children. A one stop shop in a sense for the kids to come see fascinating equipment, fire trucks, gear etc etc And of course learn about emergency services. The frontage to the public is a great platform for design features and exhibits

This small building uses a fairly simple palette of materials and is quite basic – this would service as an outpost in more rural remote setting possibly. Again, just a design I did, but the design solutions could be many

Even though small, its still like all the centres intended on being a nice design – one that carries a smart image, and like all the centres a nice place for the staff to come and work obviously

PFAC
POLICE FIRE AMBULANCE CENTR
DISASTER RESPONSE
REPORT A CRIME
PUBLIC INFORMATION
COUNSELLING
CHILDRENS CENTRE
HELP
MEDICAL EMERGENCY
FIRE EMERGENCY
RED CROSS STATION
CAFE
POLICE SECTION

FIRE SECTION
FIRE DEPT
PFAC

AMBULANCE CENTRE
POLICE SECTION

FIRE SECTION
FIRE DEPT
PFAC
POLICE SECTION

I designed this, and I really like this option for a number of reasons – it uses the basis of a prefabricated shipping container type frame with add ons. This can be mass produced and dropped anywhere easily, and moved easily too. The building itself is transported like any ship container, placed on site with a crane. This is a low cost option – good for confined areas. So this is really is in effect a police post with parking space for other services

The canopy structure gives splendour to the building and of course signals entry, as do the clip on smaller canopies. Planting and landscaping will be at everyone as well. Bold neat colours make even these small centres look smart and vibrant

The logo carries through on all the centres and appears not only on the entrance threshold, but on the floor too, just scaled down – the visuals of the logo, colours brand if you like must tie these centres all together – just as they will be digitally and in communications and data

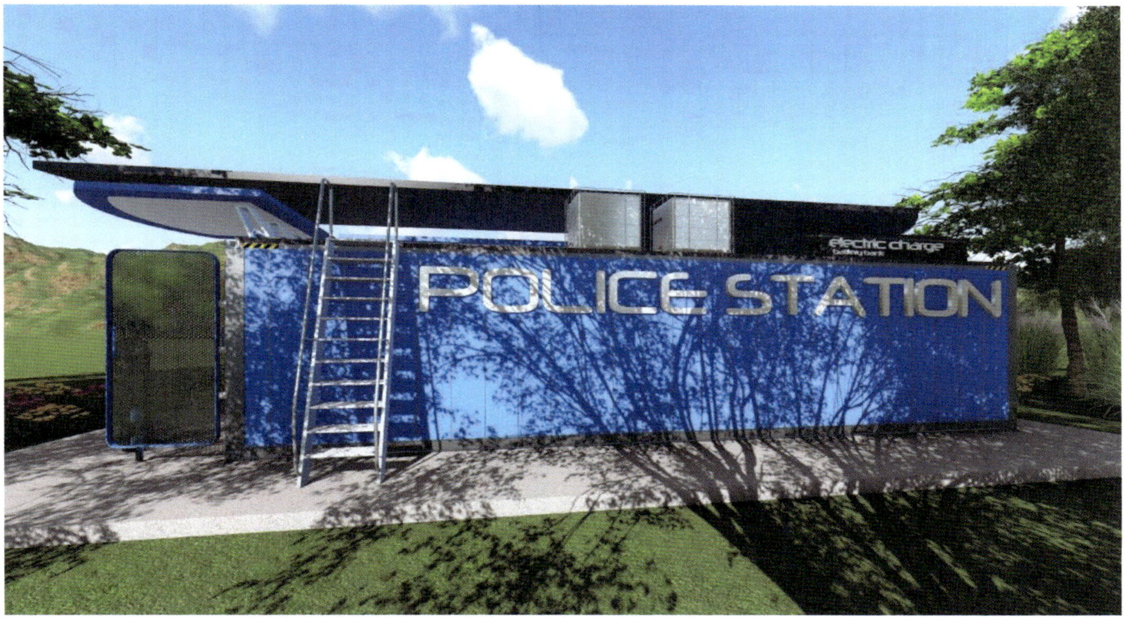
electric charge
POLICE STATION

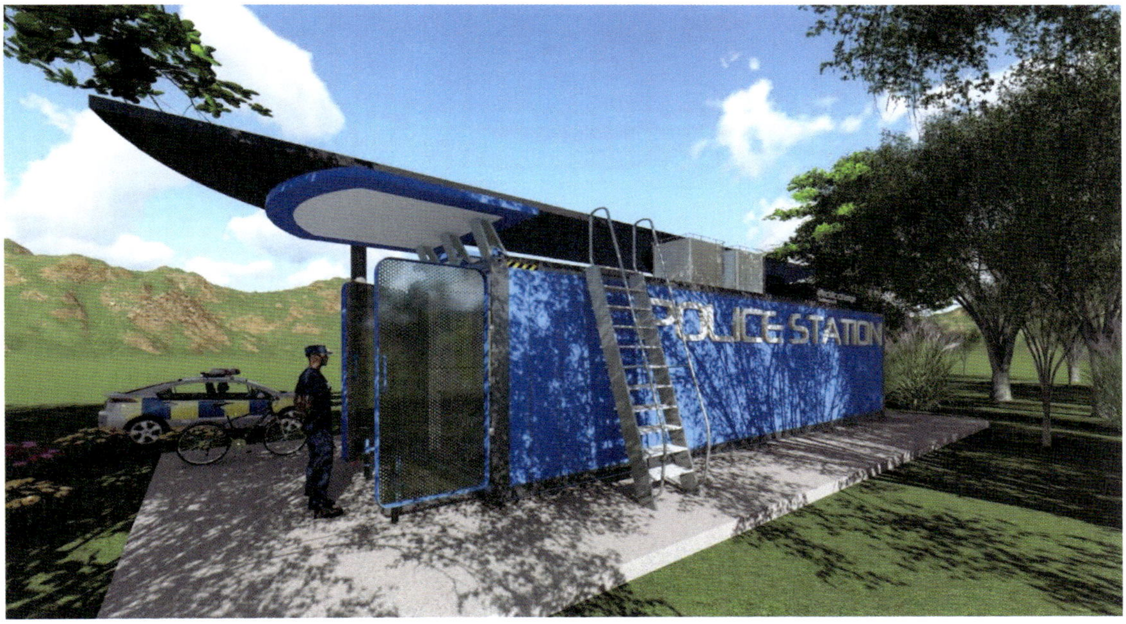
POLICE STATION

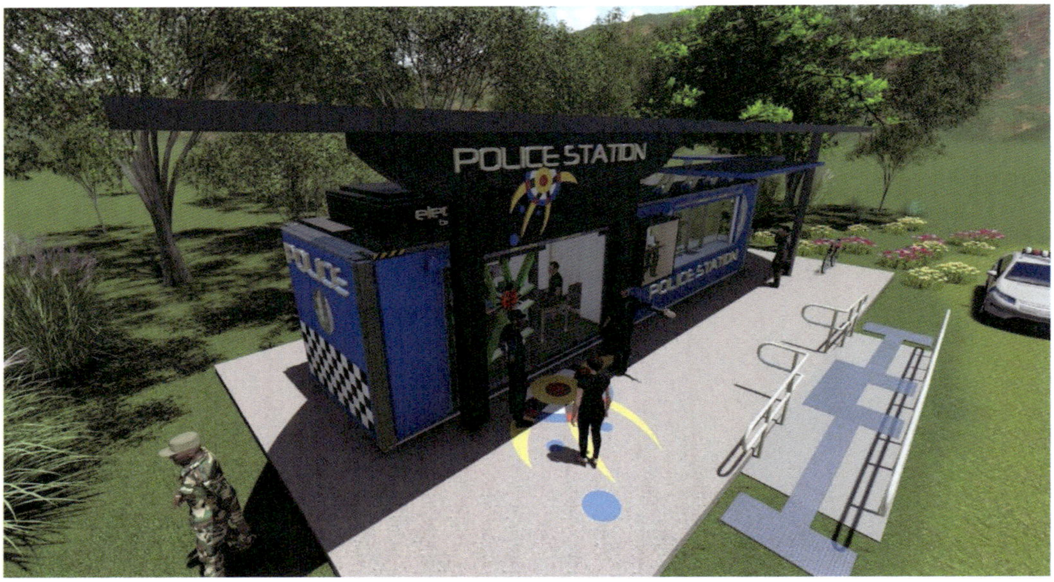
POLICE STATION
POLICE
POLICE STATION

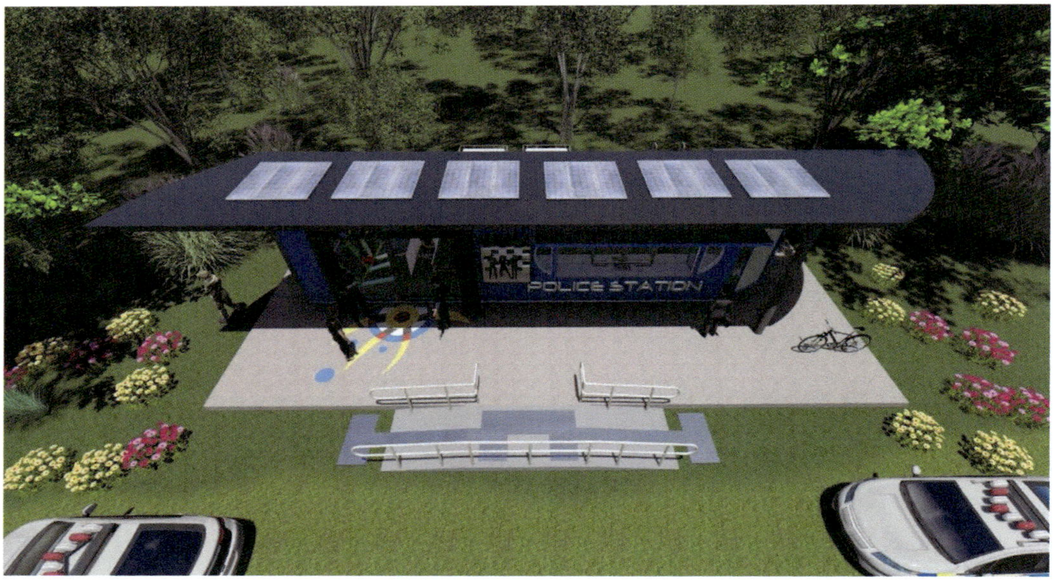
POLICE STATION

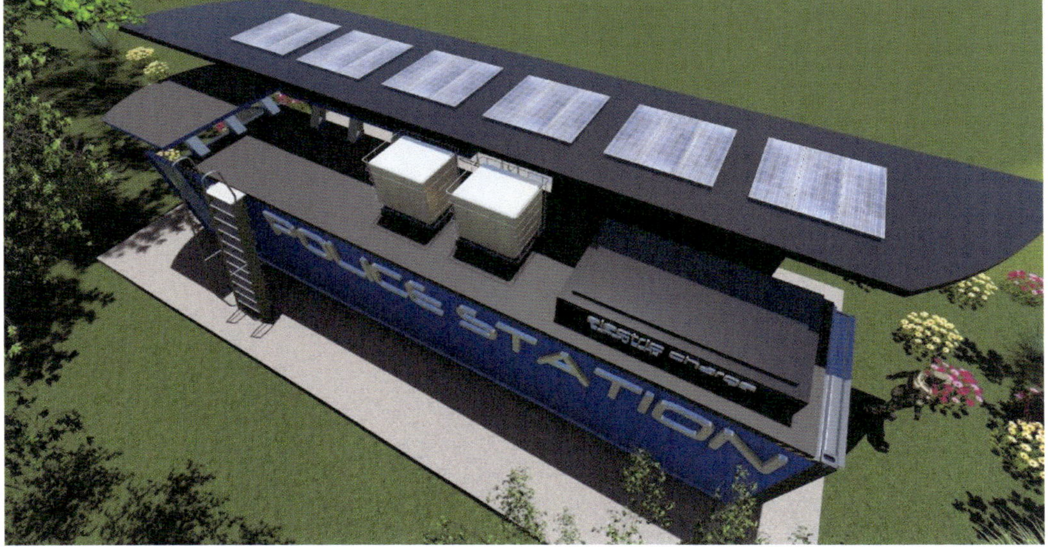
POLICE STATION

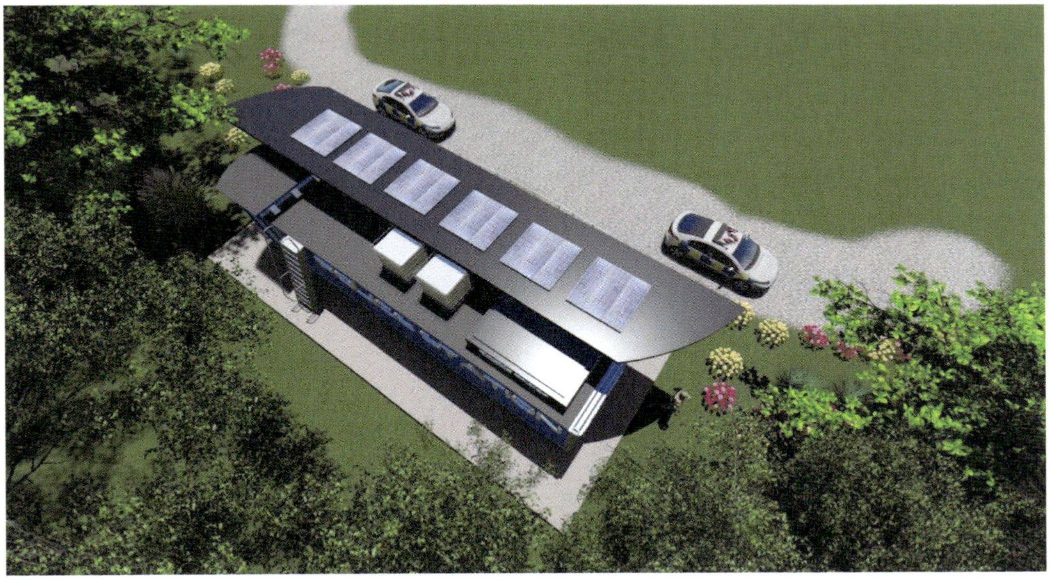

My suggestion is to think about locating these alongside 24hr accident emergency centres

Jonathan Lever
www.archilever.com

I am a qualified and registered Architect in two countries and ran my own practice in both of them. I have a reasonable background in design and buildings by default with my grandfather having been a builder, being raised learning woodwork in his workshops, then my father being an Architect who ran his own firm, with three offices in Zimbabwe and one in Mozambique. I am a keen designer too, looking at designs from small items such a pieces of furniture, right through to large scale Urban Planning interventions. Designing, creating is my hobby and passion over and above being my career. Hopefully along the way my ideas help the world. One of my slogans has kind of ended up being, helping make the world a better place. I think most of my work carries that theme somewhere in it in part. I think its important as a designer to not only have fun and enjoy being creative, but being useful and contributing something to the world is pretty important too. We all enjoyed infrastructure and technology left, created and made by others, so add on is my view.

Printed in Great Britain
by Amazon